Nita Mehta™
Cup cakes
& Brownies

Nita Mehta™

B.Sc. (Home Science), M.Sc. (Food and Nutrition) Gold Medalist

SNAB
Excellence in Books

Cup cakes
& Brownies

Snab Publishers Pvt Ltd

Corporate Office
3A/3, Asaf Ali Road, New Delhi 110 002
Phone: +91 11 2325 2948, 2325 0091
E-mail: nitamehta@nitamehta.com
Website: www.nitamehta.com

Editorial and Marketing office
E-159, Greater Kailash II, New Delhi 110 048

Food Styling and Photography by Snab
Typesetting by National Information Technology Academy
3A/3, Asaf Ali Road, New Delhi 110 002

Recipe Development & Testing:
Nita Mehta Foods - R & D Centre
3A/3, Asaf Ali Road, New Delhi - 110002

Distributed by :
NITA MEHTA BOOKS
3A/3, Asaf Ali Road, New Delhi - 02
Distribution Centre :
D16/1, Okhla Industrial Area, Phase-I,
New Delhi - 110020
Tel.: 26813199, 26813200
E-mail: nitamehta.mehta@gmail.com

Contributing Writers :
Anurag Mehta
Tanya Mehta
Subhash Mehta
Editors :
Sangeeta
Sunita

ISBN 978-81-7869-395-8

Reprint 2014

Cover Designed by: SNAB

Printed in India at Infinity Advertising Services (P) Ltd, New Delhi

Price: Rs. 295/-

Introduction

Cup cakes... the thought of making them puts my grand children into a happy mood. While they are being baked in the oven, the waiting period is filled with exciting anticipation and curiosity. The cup cakes are watched as they are gradually rising, making every minute so interesting. And once out of the oven, in a matter of minutes most of them disappear. The rewarding smiles make my day!

All recipes are quick and simple to prepare but still give delicious results. The list of ingredients for a particular recipe is not too long. There are plain cup cakes, most are frosted for an exotic taste and appeal. Others have been specially created to give the children a boost of health.

Brownies too have been included to give more value to the book. Dates, apricots, prunes etc will make these really special.

A few gluten free recipes have been given on special demand. Do pass them on to your friends who need these for gluten intolerant kids.

We hope that you'll take pleasure in the process and the many wonderful results!

Nita Mehta

CONTENTS

USEFUL EQUIPMENT...

Muffin Tray/Muffin Pan: Cup cakes and muffins are baked in a tray with depressions or cups (usually 9 or 12) in which you pour the batter. The muffin pan is lined with paper cups. While baking the cup cakes if any pan is empty always fill it with some water, so that it does not catch the naked heat of the oven.

Small Muffin Tins: Small individual cake tins which are placed on the wire rack. These are slightly deeper than the cups of the muffin pan, so the ready cakes are slightly bigger when baked in small individual tins.

Square Tin: Used for making brownies. Available in different sizes of 8", 9" or 10". For larger quantities, use rectangular baking tins.

Kitchen Weighing Balance: This is used for weighing ingredients and is a very useful device in baking. A kitchen balance can weigh upto 2 kg or upto 5 kg, normally with smaller indications worked for every 10 gms in 2 kg balance or 25 gms in a 5 kg balance. This could vary machine to machine. Place the balance at eye level and the lever at 0 level before use. Available at most crockery and utensil stores.

Electric Beater: This is a hand held machine, used for beating or whisking, for eg: butter and sugar, eggs and sugar or as per the recipe. It aids in making cakes light and fluffy and should not be substituted with a hand blender or mixers and food processors. The beater is equipped with adjustable speeds – slow to very fast.

Wooden Spoons: These are used to mix batters gently. Even broad metal spoons can be used. With spoons, the flour can be folded in an upward and downward motion or simply mixed gently.

Rubber Spatula: These are like flat spoons with a squarish rubber end. These are so flexible that they help take out all the batter from the bowl when it has to be transferred to the baking tin.

Palette Knife: This is a long knife, either flexible or firm, with no sharp edges. It is rounded or square cut at the end. It is totally flat and is used to level cream or other icings on the cake for a neater finished look. The blade of the knife is immersed in iced water to level and spread cream icings on cake. In very cold weather, the blade can be dipped in hot water to spread icings like frostings which set too quickly.

Wire Rack: This is used in the oven, to place the tin and also after baking to cool the cake. Cake should not be cooled on a plate, because this prevents steam from escaping and makes the cake soggy.

WEIGHING OR MEASURING...

Kitchen Weighing Scale

Measuring Spoons & Cups

We recommend that you weigh your ingredients using a weighing scale where ever the weight is given. Cup measure used in the recipes is the measuring cup which holds 200 ml liquid. Larger cups which hold upto 240 ml liquid are also available. Always fill the cup and level it with a knife. Do not tap before leveling it. Since different capacity cups are available, it is always better to use the weighing scale for correct measurements. However well you might beat a cake, if the proportion of the ingredients is not accurate, you might get disappointed. So, invest in a weighing scale, measuring cups and measuring spoons. However, these are the conversions...

- 1 cup maida/flour............................=115 gms
- 1 cup powdered sugar..................=125 gms
- 1 cup granulated sugar................=175 gms
- 1 cup brown sugar..........................=135 gms
- 1 cup softened yellow butter.....=180 gms
- 1 cup softened white butter.......=150 gms
- 1 cup oil..=170 gms
- 1 cup cream......................................=200 gms
- 1 cup juice/sugar syrup................=200 ml
- 1 table spoon (tbsp)......................=15 ml/gms
- 1 tea spoon (tsp).............................=5 ml/gms

MELTING CHOCOLATE...

Cooking chocolate is used in a few recipes. Moisture and strong heat are the enemies of chocolate. To melt chocolate, make a proper double boiler, so that the steam does not reach the chocolate, as steam can give moisture to the melting chocolate.

Put chopped chocolate in a steel or heat proof bowl. Place bowl on a slightly smaller pan filled with 1" water, such that the chocolate bowl can sit on the pan of water without touching the water. Keep on very low heat and wait till the chocolate softens. Remove bowl from the pan of water and stir gently with a rubber spatula to melt chocolate completely. You can also melt chocolate in a microwave. Microwave 100 gms chocolate for 30-40 seconds only till soft. Stir with a rubber spatula to melt. If needed microwave for 30 seconds more.

BAKING IN A MICROWAVE...

A microwave oven on microwave mode cannot be used for baking any contents of this book. Only the convection mode of the microwave can be used for baking. So, only if your microwave has a convection mode, you can bake these cakes. When the microwave is on the convection mode, there are no microwaves travelling inside the microwave. Hence, all dishes and tins which go into the conventional OTG can very safely be used in the microwave. Metal cake tins, aluminium foil for covering or heat proof glass dishes work very well in the microwave when it is on the convection mode. To use the microwave oven for baking, set the needed temperature using the 'Convec button'. Press 'Start' to preheat the microwave oven. When the oven is heated to the desired temperature, it will give a beep. Do not press 'Stop'. Simply open the door, place the cake on the wire rack and close the door. Set the 'time' needed to bake the cake. Press 'Start'. The cake now starts to get baked in the preheated oven at the set temperature and for the set time needed for baking.

HANDY BAKING TIPS...

- All ingredients should be at room temperature for best results.
- Check expiry dates of ingredients, especially essences, baking powder and soda-bi-carb before use.
- Sift dry ingredients well, so that the mixture is aerated.
- Use the correct size baking tin. For muffin pans, line with paper cups or grease muffin pan with oil and then dust with flour to prevent sticking of cup cakes.
- Always line the brownie tin with parchment or baking paper. Regular plain paper can be used but it needs to be greased lightly. When brownies are removed from the oven, wait for 10-15 minutes before removing the paper. The paper sticks too much and is difficult to remove if not removed once the brownie cools slightly.
- Never fill muffin pans more than ¾ of the cup. A prepared cake mixture should go straight into the hot oven. Always bake in the centre of the oven.
- When the recipe calls for 'beating', use an electric hand beater to beat the mixture till light and fluffy. If the recipe says to 'mix using a spoon', just mix all ingredients till well combined. Do not overmix or overbeat.
- Do not beat the batter after the flour has been added or the finished cake will turn out heavy. Simply use a spoon to fold the flour in.
- Let the cup cakes cool in the muffin cup for 5 minutes before removing them to a rack to cool.
- Always preheat oven to required temperature before baking.

Favourite

CUP CAKES

Red Velvet Cup cakes

Makes 12

Ingredients

1⅓ cups (150 gms) flour (*maida*)
½ tsp baking soda (*mitha soda*)
½ tsp baking powder
¼ tsp salt, 1 cup caster sugar
¼ cup butter, room temperature
1 egg
1 tsp vanilla essence, 1 tbsp unsweetened cocoa powder, sifted
1 tsp raspberry red food colouring
1 cup buttermilk (¼ cup yogurt + ¾ cup milk)

VANILLA CREAM CHEESE FROSTING

½ cup cream cheese/cheese spread, room temperature
½ cup unsalted butter, room temperature
1 tsp vanilla essence, 1 cup icing sugar, or to taste

Method

1. Preheat oven at 180°C/350°F. Line a 12 cup muffin tin with paper liners.

2. In a medium bowl, whisk together flour, baking soda, baking powder and salt.

3. In a large bowl, beat together butter and sugar until light. Beat in the egg and vanilla essence.

4. Sift in the cocoa powder, add in red food coloring and mix everything until well combined on low speed.

5. Gradually add half of the flour mixture followed by half of the buttermilk. Mix well. Add half of the remaining flour mixture, followed by all the remaining buttermilk Add the last of the flour. Mix just until no streaks of dry ingredients remain. Do not over mix.

6. Divide batter evenly into prepared muffin cups.

7. Bake for 20 minutes, or until a toothpick inserted into the center of a cup cake comes out clean. Turn cup cakes out onto a wire rack to cool completely before frosting.

8. In a large bowl, beat all ingredients except the icing sugar. Gradually blend in the sugar until the icing is smooth and creamy. Check sweetness. Spread or pipe onto cooled cup cakes.

Note: If you can sacrifice one cup cake, crumble it and put these cake crumbs in the microwave for 2 minutes to dry. Sprinkle on the frosting.

Chocolate Brownie Cup cakes

Makes 10-12

Ingredients

¾ cup flour (*maida*)
½ cup cocoa powder
1 tsp baking powder
¼ tsp salt
½ cup caster sugar
½ cup brown sugar
¾ cup butter, melted and cooled slightly
½ tsp vanilla essence
½ tsp almond essence
3 eggs
½ cup chocolate chips

CHOCOLATE BUTTER CREAM
100 gm unsalted butter, softened
200 gm icing sugar
½ tsp vanilla essence
40 gm cocoa powder, or as desired
few yellow or silver balls for decoration

Method

1. Preheat oven to 180°C/350°F. Line a muffin pan with paper cups.

2. In a small bowl, mix together flour, cocoa powder, baking powder and salt.

3. In a large bowl, whisk together caster sugar, brown sugar and butter until smooth. Whisk in vanilla and almond essence. Add eggs, one at a time, beating well after each addition. Add flour mixture, beating until combined. Stir in chocolate chips.

4. Scoop batter into prepared pan. Bake in preheated oven for 20-25 minutes or until a tooth pick inserted into center comes out with a few crumbs attached and a little melted chocolate. The tops of cup cakes will not spring back when touched.

5. Let cool in pan on rack for 10 minutes. Remove from pan and let cool completely on rack.

6. For chocolate butter cream, mix cocoa powder with 2 tbsp water to make a smooth paste and keep aside. Beat together the butter, icing sugar and vanilla until smooth. Add the chocolate paste. Add enough to get a nice colour. Put it in a piping bag and pipe big stars over the cooled cup cakes forming a heap in the centre. Decorate with coloured balls.

Chocolate Chip Cup cakes

Makes 8

Ingredients

100 gm butter
100 gm caster sugar
2 eggs
120 gm flour (*maida*)
½ tsp vanilla essence
1/8 tsp lemon juice
¼ tsp baking powder
60 gm choco chip

Method

1. Sieve flour and baking powder.

2. Beat butter and sugar till fluffy and creamy. Add essence and lemon juice and beat well.

3. Add 2 tbsp flour and beat well, add the eggs one at a time and beat well.

4. Fold in the remaining flour. Dust the chips in 1 tbsp flour and mix into the batter, keeping 2 tbsp separate.

5. Line a muffin tray with paper cups and fill each till ¾, sprinkle the dusted chips.

6. Bake in a preheated oven at 180ºC/350°F for 20 minutes.

Double Chocolate Chip Cup cakes

These are chocolate cup cakes with chocolate chips. So use 20 gm cocoa and reduce flour to 100 gm instead of 120 gm flour. Sift cocoa along with the flour.

Marble Choco Vanilla Cup cakes

Makes 15

Ingredients

180 gm flour (*maida*)
1½ tsp baking powder
180 gm unsalted butter, softened
180 gm caster sugar
3 eggs
2 tbsp cocoa powder
2 tbsp water
1 tsp vanilla essence
icing sugar, for dusting

Method

1. Preheat the oven at 180°C/350°F.

2. Sift the flour and baking powder into a large bowl and add the butter, caster sugar and eggs. Beat well until the mixture is smooth. Transfer half the mixture to a separate bowl.

3. Mix the cocoa powder with water and stir into one bowl of mixture. Add the vanilla essence to the other bowl and mix evenly.

4. Spoon alternate tablespoons of the two mixtures into the prepared cups and swirl lightly with a fork for a marbled effect.

5. Bake in the preheated oven for 20 minutes., or until risen, firm and golden brown. Leave to cool in the tin for 10 minutes, then turn out and finish cooling on a wire rack. If you like, you can decorate them with different flavours of butter cream as given under rainbow cup cakes on page 24.

Chocolate Fudge Cup cakes

Makes 12

Ingredients

1 cup flour (*maida*)
½ cup cocoa powder
1 tsp baking powder
¼ tsp salt
1 cup caster sugar
½ cup oil
1 tsp vanilla essence
3 eggs
½ cup chopped chocolate

CHOCOLATE FUDGE FROSTING
150 gm chocolate - chopped
100 gm unsalted butter, softened
120 gm icing sugar
1½ tsp vanilla essence

Method

1. Preheat oven to 180°C/350°F and use muffin pan lined with paper cups.

2. In a small bowl, mix together flour, cocoa powder, baking powder and salt.

3. In a large bowl, whisk together sugar and oil for 2 minutes. Whisk in vanilla.

4. Add eggs, one at a time, beating well after each addition.

5. Add flour mixture, beating until combined.

6. Add chocolate and mix lightly with a spatula.

7. Scoop batter into prepared pan. Bake in preheated oven for 20 minutes or until a tooth pick inserted into center comes out with a few crumbs attached and a little melted chocolate. The tops of cup cakes will not spring back when touched.

8. Let cool in pan on rack for 10 minutes. Remove from pan and let cool completely on rack.

9. For chocolate fudge frosting, melt chocolate in a double boiler (see page 7) or microwave for 30 seconds. Stir well with a spatula to make it smooth and keep aside. Beat together the butter, icing sugar and vanilla until smooth and fluffy. Add the melted chocolate and beat at low speed till incorporated. Now beat on high speed till smooth and glossy. Put it in a piping bag and pipe over the cooled cup cakes.

Nutty Coffee Cup cakes

Makes 16

Ingredients

180 gm flour (*maida*), 1½ tsp baking powder
180 gm unsalted butter softened
180 gm light brown sugar
3 eggs
2 tsp coffee mixed with 1 tbsp water
50 gm almonds or walnuts, chopped
1 tbsp raisins
4 tbsp honey, optional

Method

1. Preheat the oven at 180°C/350°F. Line a regular size muffin tin with paper cups.

2. Sift the flour and baking powder into a large bowl and add the butter, sugar, eggs and coffee. Beat well until the mixture is smooth, then stir in the chopped walnuts/almonds and raisins.

3. Spoon the mixture into the prepared cups. Bake in the preheated oven for 20-25 minutes, or until risen, firm and golden brown.

4. Leave to cool in the tin for 10 minutes, then turn out carefully onto a wire rack. Whilst the cake is still warm, spoon over half the honey. Leave to cool completely. To serve, drizzle over the remaining honey and top with raisins.

Spiced Apple Cup cakes

Makes 12

Ingredients

1 cup grated apple, with skin
1 cup sugar, ¾ cup water
¾ cup butter, 1 egg
1 tsp cinnamon (*dalchini*)
½ tsp nutmeg (*jaiphal*)
¼ tsp ground cloves (*laung*)
1¾ cups flour (*maida*)
1 tsp baking powder
½ tsp baking soda (*mitha soda*)

Method

1. Preheat oven to 180°C/350°F.

2. Line muffin pan with paper cups.

3. Put the grated apples, sugar, water, butter, cinnamon, nutmeg and cloves into a large saucepan and bring to a boil.

4. Cool add egg, flour, baking powder and baking soda.

5. Fill paper lined cup cake tins 2/3 full.

6. Bake for 20-25 minutes until cup cakes spring back when touched in the center.

Jam & Coconut Cup cakes

Makes 16

Ingredients

180 gm flour (*maida*), 1½ tsp baking powder, 1 tbsp custard powder
180 gm unsalted butter, softened
180 gm caster sugar, 3 eggs
1 tsp vanilla essence
mixed fruit jam, 1 cup desiccated coconut for topping

MASCARPONE FROSTING
200 gm whipping cream, 200 gm mascarpone
1 cup icing sugar, or to taste
1 tsp vanilla essence

Method

1. Preheat the oven to 180°C/350°F. Place paper cups into muffin pan.

2. Sift the flour, baking powder and custard powder into a large bowl and add the butter, caster sugar, eggs and vanilla. Beat well until the mixture is smooth.

3. Divide the mixture between the paper cups and place a half teaspoon of jam on to the centre of each, without pressing down.

4. Bake in the preheated oven for 20-25 minutes, or until risen, firm and golden brown. Transfer the cup cakes to a wire rack to cool completely.

5. For the frosting, beat cream in a bowl with an electric hand beater till soft peaks form. Do not over beat. In a separate bowl, beat mascarpone, sugar and vanilla essence until smooth. Fold the whipped cream with a spatula into the mascarpone mixture.

6. Spread the frosting over the cold cup cakes, making a neat dome shape. Roll the tops of the cup cakes over desiccated coconut spread on a plate to coat completely.

Special
CUP CAKES

Rainbow Cup cakes

Serves 16

Ingredients

180 gm flour (*maida*)
1½ tsp baking powder
180 gm unsalted butter, softened
180 gm caster sugar
3 eggs
1 tsp vanilla essence
coloured sprinkles, to decorate

VANILLA BUTTER CREAM
100 gm unsalted butter, softened
200 gm icing sugar
½ tsp vanilla essence

CHOCOLATE BUTTER CREAM
100 gm unsalted butter, softened
200 gm icing sugar
½ tsp vanilla essence
40 gm cocoa powder, or as desired

Method

1. Preheat the oven to 180°C/350°F and place paper cups in a muffin pan.

2. Sift the flour and baking powder into a large bowl and add the butter, caster sugar, eggs and vanilla. Beat well until the mixture is smooth, then stir in enough of the milk to make a soft dropping consistency.

3. Divide the mixture between the paper cups. Bake in the preheated oven for 20 minutes, or until risen, firm and golden brown. Transfer the cup cakes to a wire rack to cool.

4. For the butter cream, beat together the butter, icing sugar and vanilla until smooth. For chocolate butter cream, mix cocoa powder with 2 tbsp water to make a smooth paste and add to the above icing.

5. Spread or pipe a little of the butter cream on top of each cake. Decorate with the coloured sprinkles.

Coffee Cup cakes

Serves 16

Ingredients

180 gm flour (*maida*)
1½ tsp baking powder
180 gm unsalted butter, softened
180 gm caster sugar
3 eggs
2 tsp coffee mixed with 1 tbsp water
2 tbsp milk

FROSTING
55 gm unsalted butter
115 gm brown sugar
2 tbsp milk
½ tsp coffee mixed with little water
400 gm icing sugar sifted
cocoa powder for dusting

Method

1. Preheat the oven to 190ºC/375ºF. Place paper cups into a muffin tray.

2. Sift the flour and baking powder into a large bowl and add the butter, caster sugar, eggs and coffee. Beat well until the mixture is smooth, then beat in the milk.

3. Divide the mixture between the paper cups. Bake in the preheated oven for 20-25 minutes, or until risen, firm and golden brown. Transfer the cup cakes to a wire rack to cool.

4. For the frosting, place the butter, sugar, milk and coffee in a saucepan over a medium heat and stir until melted and smooth. Bring to the boil. Keep boiling continuously for 2 minutes, stirring constantly. Remove from heat and beat in the icing sugar.

5. Stir the frosting until smooth and thick, then spoon into a piping bag fitted with a big nozzle. Pipe a swirl of frosting on top of each cup cakes and dust with cocoa powder.

Cherry Cup cakes with Ricotta

Makes 16

Ingredients

180 gm flour (*maida*)
70 gm glace cherries - chopped
1½ tsp baking powder
1 tbsp cornflour
180 gm unsalted butter softened
180 gm caster sugar
3 eggs
1 tsp vanilla essence
glace cherries, to decorate (optional)

FROSTING
250 gm ricotta cheese OR 200 gm paneer
    mixed with 50 gm cream
70 gm icing sugar, or o taste
½ tsp vanilla essence
pink food colour, optional
3-4 glace cherries - very finely chopped

Method

1. Preheat the oven to 190°C/375°F. Place paper cups into tin.

2. Stir a tablespoon of the flour into the chopped glace cherries. Sift the remaining flour with the baking powder and cornflour into a large bowl and add the butter, caster sugar, eggs and vanilla. Beat well until the mixture is smooth, then stir in the glace cherries and flour mixture.

3. Divide the mixture between the paper cups. Bake in the preheated oven for 15-20 minutes, or until risen, firm and golden brown. Transfer the cup cakes to a wire rack to cool.

4. For the frosting, put ricotta or cream and paneer with the icing sugar and vanilla in a small grinder and blend till smooth. Spoon a little on top of each cup cake. Top each with a cherry. For a pink cherry frosting, colour the icing with pink colour and add a few finely chopped cherries.

Truffle Cup cakes with Feather Effect

Makes 16

Ingredients

CHOCOLATE CUP CAKES

160 gm flour (*maida*)
20 gm cocoa powder, 2 tbsp water
1½ tsp baking powder
180 gm unsalted butter, softened
180 gm caster sugar
3 eggs
1 tsp vanilla essence

TRUFFLE ICING

150 gm cream
300 gm dark cooking chocolate

DECORATION (FEATHER EFFECT)

50 gm white chocolate melted and put in a paper cone
a few cherries

Method

1. For the cup cakes, preheat the oven to 180°C/350°F. Place paper cups into tin.

2. Sift the flour and baking powder into a large bow.

3. Add the butter, sugar, eggs and vanilla essence. Beat well until the mixture is smooth.

4. Mix the water with the cocoa powder to make a smooth paste and stir into the mixture.

5. Divide the mixture between the paper cups. Bake in the preheated oven for 20 minutes, or until risen, firm from top. Transfer the cup cakes to a wire rack to cool.

6. To make truffle icing, heat cream in a heavy bottom pan on low heat till it becomes hot. Do not let it boil. Add chocolate to it. Mix nicely to remove any lumps. Remove from fire when almost melted and mix well. Let it cool to room temperature. Keep aside.

7. After the cup cakes are cool, pour the truffle on each so that the cup cakes are covered with it evenly.

8. Melt white chocolate as given on page 7. Put into a paper cone and draw 4-5 horizontal lines at an interval of ½" on half of the iced cake. While the lines are still wet, run a toothpick vertically in the opposite direction, through the white lines to get a feather effect. Decorate with a cherry.

Fondant Celebration Cup cakes

Makes 16

Ingredients

FONDANT
½ kg (4 cups) icing sugar
25 ml water - approx. (2-3 tbsp)
8 gm (3 tsp) gelatine, 80 gm (¼ cup) liquid glucose
½ tsp glycerin
15 gm (1 tbsp) margarine or unsalted butter
flavoring - as desired, colour - as desired

VANILLA CUP CAKES
180 gm flour, 1½ tsp baking powder
180 gm unsalted butter, softened
180 gm caster sugar, 3 eggs
1 tsp vanilla essence

TO DECORATE
colored balls, silver balls, hundred thousand and other sprinkles

Method

1. For the fondant, sieve icing sugar and keep aside in a kneading bowl.

2. Take water in a small pan and sprinkle gelatine over it. Let it soak. Melt on low heat.

3. Melt butter or margarine on low heat in a pan. Remove from heat when melted. Add glucose, glycerin, melted gelatine and essence .

4. Add gelatine-margarine mixture to the sugar and knead into a smooth dough. If dough appears hard, sprinkle some water and knead the dough. Wrap fondant in a plastic/cling wrap and rest for 8-10 hours at room temperature. Add colour as desired at the time of use.

5. For the cup cakes, preheat the oven to 180°C/350°F. Place paper cups into tins or put double-layer paper cups on to the baking trays.

6. Sift the flour and baking powder into a large bowl and add the butter, caster sugar, eggs and vanilla.

7. Beat well until the mixture is smooth and is of a soft dropping consistency. Divide the mixture between the paper cups. Bake in the preheated oven for 20 minutes, or until risen, firm and golden brown. Transfer the cup cakes to a wire rack to cool.

8. To cover a cup cake, add colour as desired. Roll out thinly, using cornflour for dusting. Cut out rounds with a cookie cutter, big enough to cover the top of the cup cake. Stick using a little water. Decorate with fondant roses and leaves and coloured balls as given on page 32.

Making a Rose with Fondant

1. Colour ¾ of the fondant for roses and ¼ of it for green leaves.

2. For a rose, roll out a small ball on a surface. Cut into 2 pieces. Roll each piece gently into a cone with a finger to get 2 centres.

3. Roll out more balls and cut each into half. Wrap these as petals around the cone centre, keeping the cut side at the base of the centre and pressing the petal to the centre cone to secure. Remember to keep the height of the petal slightly more than the centre. Repeat with more petals, each overlapping. Make the next row of petals slightly bigger until the required size is achieved. When you press the petal to the centre, press only at the base to secure. Keep the upper part of the petal free. Bend back the top ends of the larger petals to curl. Cut the extra base of the rose if any and reuse.

4. For leaves, make balls and shape them into long and pointed rolls. Roll out and cut with a leaf cutter. Alternately, flatten a ball of fondant with the palm to make leaves and mark veins with a knife. Bend the leaf slightly to give a natural effect.

Other Fondant Flowers

1. Make fondant as given. Divide into 2 portions. Colour one part pink, the other yellow. Roll out the pink coloured fondant thinly. Loosen with a knife. Immediately, cut small flowers with a small flower cutter.

2. Roll out the yellow paste and cut it also in the same way, keeping the size a little bigger or smaller than the pink ones. Cut more flowers of different sizes and place them one on top of another on a cup cake covered with fondant.

Snow Man Cup cakes

Makes 16-18

Ingredients

chocolate cup cakes - page 28 or vanilla cup cakes - page 30
fondant - page 30
some sugar crystals

BUTTER-CREAM ICING

150 gm butter (unsalted), 200 gm icing sugar, 1 tsp vanilla essence
2 tbsp condensed milk, few drops of lemon juice
blue food colour

Method

1. Make fondant as given on page 30.

2. Bake cup cakes and let them cool.

3. To prepare butter icing, beat butter, icing sugar and essence together for 2-3 minutes. Add condensed milk and lemon juice. Beat again for 2-3 minutes till fluffy. Add colour and mix well.

4. Put butter icing in an icing bag and pipe on the cup cake to cover the top. Sprinkle sugar crystals.

5. Colour fondant as shown for snow man and make snow men. Arrange on the iced cup cakes.

Strawberry Ripple Cup cakes

Serves 16

Ingredients

180 gm flour, 1½ tsp baking powder, 1 tbsp cornflour
180 gm unsalted butter, softened
180 gm caster sugar, 3 eggs, 1 tsp strawberry essence
200 gm fresh strawberries or ½ cup strawberry crush

CREAM CHEESE FROSTING
50 gm unsalted butter, 200 gm cream cheese, 150 gm icing sugar

Method

1. Preheat the oven to 190ºC/375ºF. Place paper cups into muffin tin.

2. Sift the flour, baking powder and cornflour into a large bowl and add the butter, caster sugar, eggs and essence. Beat well until the mixture is smooth.

3. Mash the strawberries lightly with a fork, then fold into the mixture, if using crush then lightly swirl the crush into the batter (Do not over mix)

4. Divide the mixture between the paper cups. Bake in the preheated oven for 20-25 minutes, or until risen, firm and golden brown. Transfer the cup cakes to a wire rack to cool.

5. For the frosting, beat butter till soft. Add cream cheese and beat on low speed for 2 minutes. Gradually add sugar into the bowl and beat for 2-3 minutes till smooth and glossy. Check sweetness and add more sugar if required. Refrigerate for 45 minutes or till firm enough to pipe.

Lunch Box
CUP CAKES

Corn Cup cakes

Makes 12

Ingredients

½ cup (90 gm) butter
½ cup + 2 tbsp sugar
¼ cup honey
2 eggs
½ tsp salt
1½ cups flour (*maida*)
¾ cup cornmeal (*makki ka atta*)
½ tsp baking powder
½ cup milk
¾ cup frozen corn

Method

1. Preheat oven to 180°C/350°F.

2. Mix butter, sugar, honey, eggs and salt into a large bowl.

3. Add flour, cornmeal and baking powder and blend thoroughly.

4. Add milk while mixing.

5. Add corn to mixture and mix well.

6. Do not mash corn, the whole kernel is baked into the cup cake.

7. Fill a muffin pan with 12 paper cups and fill 2/3 full with batter.

8. Bake for 20-25 minutes or till golden brown.

Country Fruit Cup cakes

Makes 20

Ingredients

175 gm flour (*maida*), 60 gm whole-wheat flour (*atta*)
2 tsp baking powder, ½ tsp ground nutmeg (*jaiphal*)
240 gm unsalted butter, softened
240 gm sugar
4 eggs, 1 tsp vanilla essence
2 tbsp raisins, ½ cup candied fruit or chopped glace cherries
2 tbsp flaked almonds
1 tbsp brown sugar to top

Method

1. Sift the flours, baking powder and nutmeg into a large bowl, adding any bran left in the sieve. Add the butter, sugar, eggs and vanilla essence. Beat well until the mixture is smooth. Add 1 tbsp milk if the batter appears too thick. It should be of a soft dropping consistency. Stir in the raisins and candied fruit.

2. Spoon the mixture into muffin tray lined with paper cups. Top with flaked almonds. Sprinkle brown sugar evenly over the surface. Bake in the preheated oven at 160°C/325°F for 30-35 minutes or until risen, firm and golden brown.

3. Leave to cool in the cups for about 10 minutes, then turn out and finish cooling on a wire rack.

Cola Cup cakes with Nutella

Makes 10-12

Ingredients

¾ cup + 1 tbsp flour (*maida*)
¾ cup caster sugar
1/3 cup cocoa, measured, then sifted
½ tsp baking soda (*mitha soda*)
½ tsp baking powder
pinch of salt
½ tsp vanilla
1 egg
¼ cup oil
¼ cup cola
¼ cup yogurt

CREAMY NUTELLA TOPPING
¾ cup nutella (chocolate spread)
1 cup unsalted butter, softened
2 cups icing sugar
½ tsp vanilla essence
some chocolate vermicelli

Method

1. Preheat oven to 180°C/350°F.

2. Line muffin tins with paper cups.

3. In a large bowl, using a wire whisk, stir together flour, caster sugar, cocoa, soda, baking powder and salt.

4. In a bowl, mix all wet ingredients - vanilla, egg, oil, cola and yogurt. Add these wet ingredients to the above dry mixture, using a large wire whisk, or beat with electric hand beater on medium speed for 1-2 minutes to get a thick pouring batter. If needed, add 1-2 tbsp cola to get a thick pouring batter.

5. Pour into prepared pan. Bake for 25-30 minutes or until cooked. Cup cakes should be slightly puffed up in centre and spring back when touched. Leave on a wire rack to cool completely.

6. For nutella topping, beat butter till smooth. Add icing sugar and vanilla and beat again until smooth and fluffy. Add the nutella chocolate paste. Add enough to get a nice colour. Put it in a piping bag and pipe over the cooled cup cakes. Sprinkle some chocolate vermicelli.

Zucchini Cup cakes

Makes-20

Ingredients

2 eggs
1¼ cups caster sugar
½ cup oil
½ cup orange juice
1 tsp almond essence or vanilla essence
1½ cups flour (*maida*), 1 cup whole wheat flour (*atta*)
2 tsp ground cinnamon (*dalchini*)
½ tsp ground cloves (*laung*)
2 tsp baking powder
1 tsp baking soda (*mitha soda*)
½ tsp salt
1½ cups grated zucchini

Method

1. In a mixing bowl, beat eggs, sugar, oil, orange juice and essence.

2. Combine dry ingredients and add to the egg mixture and beat well.

3. Add grated zucchini and mix well.

4. Fill greased or paper-lined muffins cups two-third full.

5. Bake at 180ºC/350ºF for 20-25 minutes or until cup cakes test done.

6. Cool for 10 minutes before removing to a wire rack.

Healthy Honey Banana Cup cakes

Makes 10

Ingredients

1 cup whole wheat flour (*atta*), ¾ cup flour (*maida*)
1 tsp baking soda (*mitha soda*), ½ tsp salt
1 tsp vanilla essence
2 tbsp wheat germ (optional)
1/3 cup oil
½ cup honey
2 eggs
1 cup mashed ripe banana (2 bananas)
¼ cup hot water

Method

1. Stir together dry ingredients.

2. Beat oil and honey together, add eggs and beat well.

3. Mash bananas. Add bananas to the cake mix and beat to combine.

4. Add dry ingredients, alternating with hot water, mix well after each addition.

5. Spoon batter into 10 greased muffin cups. Bake at 160ºC/325ºF for 25 minutes, or until muffins are golden brown and test done. Remove from oven and cool on rack.

Garlic Onion Savoury Cup cakes

Makes 12

Ingredients

2 cups (230 gm) flour (*maida*)
3 tsp baking powder
¾ tsp salt
3 tbsp sugar
1 egg beaten
1 cup milk
¼ cup melted butter
2 garlic cloves crushed
1 medium onion - finely chopped

Method

1. Heat oven to 200°C/400°F.

2. In a large bowl, mix flour, baking powder, salt and sugar.

3. In a small bowl, mix together egg, milk, garlic and onion.

4. Make a well in the center of dry ingredients and pour in the egg mixture and melted butter.

5. Mix together using as few stokes as possible.

6. Do not over beat the batter, it should have small lumps in it.

7. Pour into 12 paper-lined muffins tins, filling about 2/3 full.

8. Bake for 20 minutes or until muffins begin to turn golden on top.

9. Test for doneness with a toothpick which should come out clean.

10. Remove from tins and cool slightly before serving.

Choco Cup cakes

Makes 16-18

Ingredients

180 gm flour (*maida*)
1½ tsp baking powder
180 gm unsalted butter, softened
180 gm caster sugar
3 eggs
1 tsp vanilla essence
2 tbsp milk
1 tbsp cocoa - powder
1 cup chocos - crumbled
3 tbsp apricot jam, warmed

Method

1. Preheat the oven to 190°C/375°F. Place paper cups into tin.

2. Sift the flour and baking powder into a large bowl and add the butter, sugar, eggs and vanilla essence. Beat well until the mixture is smooth. Mix the milk with the cocoa powder and stir into the mixture.

3. Divide the mixture between the paper cups and sprinkle each with about 1 tbsp of the crumbled chocos. Bake in the preheated oven for 15-20 minutes, or until risen, firm and golden brown. Transfer the cup cakes to a wire rack to cool.

4. When the cup cakes are cold brush the tops with apricot jam and sprinkle with the remaining crumbled chocos.

Note: You may top cup cakes with honey cornflakes, muessili or any other flavoured and sweetened cornflakes.

Banana Oat Carrot Cup cakes

Makes 18

Ingredients

>1 cup grated carrots
>3-5 ripe bananas
>½ cup firmly packed brown sugar
>2 eggs
>½ cup melted butter
>1 tsp vanilla essence
>1½ cups flour (*maida*)
>1 cup quick-cooking oats
>1½ tsp baking powder
>1½ tsp baking soda (*mitha soda*)

Method

1. Mash bananas into grated carrots to equal 2½ cups, (there should be a few lumps of bananas)

2. Add sugar and eggs.

3. Mix in melted butter and essence.

4. In separate bowl combine dry ingredients - flour, oats, baking powder and baking soda.

5. Add dry ingredients to wet ingredients and mix until incorporated.

6. Grease and dust muffin cups with flour. Alternately use paper cups.

7. Bake in a preheated oven at 180ºC for 20-30 minutes or until toothpick comes clean.

8. Let rest for 5 minutes.

9. Remove from pan to cooling racks.

Fruity & Nutty
CUP CAKES

Ginger Bread Cup cakes

Serves 18-20

Ingredients

180 gm flour (*maida*)
1½ tsp baking powder
2 tsp ground ginger
1 tsp ground cinnamon
180 gm unsalted butter softened
180 gm brown sugar
3 eggs
1 tsp vanilla essence
chopped crystallized ginger or cherries to decorate

FROSTING
50 gm unsalted butter, softened
150 gm icing sugar - sifted
2-3 tbsp orange juice

Method

1. Preheat the oven to 190°C/375°F. Place paper cups into tray.

2. Sift the flour, baking powder, ginger and cinnamon into a large bowl and add the butter, sugar, eggs and vanilla extract. Beat well until the mixture is smooth.

3. Divide the mixture between the paper cups. Bake in the preheated oven for about 20 minutes, or until risen, firm and golden brown. Transfer the cup cakes to a wire rack to cool.

4. For the frosting, beat together the butter and icing sugar. Add enough orange juice and beat until smooth of a piping consistency. Spoon or pipe a little frosting on top of each cup cake and top with the crystalised ginger or a cherry.

Banana Marble Cup cakes

Makes 8-9

Ingredients

1 cup flour (*maida*), ½ cup granulated sugar ¼ cup cocoa

¾ tsp baking powder, ¼ tsp baking soda, a pinch salt

1 egg

¼ cup milk, approx

½ cup banana, mashed (1 large ripe banana)

¼ cup oil, 1 tsp vanilla essence

MARBLE FROSTING

85 gm unsalted butter, softened

150 gm icing sugar - sifted

1 tsp vanilla essence

½ cup chopped chocolate (60 gm) or 20 gm

cocoa dissolved in 2 tbsp hot water

Method

1. Mash banana with a fork in a medium bowl. Add egg, milk, oil and vanilla.

2. In another big mixing bowl, combine all the remaining dry ingredients.

3. Add liquid ingredients into dry ingredients and mix lightly with a spatula.

4. Line muffin tray with paper cups. Fill ¾ full. Bake at 190°C/375°F for 18 minutes or until a toothpick comes out clean. Cool 5 minutes before removing from tray to cool on wire racks. Let cool completely.

5. For the frosting, melt chocolate on a double boiler as on page 7 or microwave for 20 seconds. Stir to melt and keep aside. Beat together the butter and icing sugar until smooth and fluffy. Transfer half of it carefully in a piping bag, spooning it from the side . To the remaining half of the icing add melted chocolate or cocoa paste and mix well. Spoon this chocolate frosting in the same piping bag carefully from the other side of the bag, so as not to mix them. Pipe on cooled cup cakes to get vanilla and chocolate frosting together.

Carrot Pineapple Cup cakes

Makes 10-12

Ingredients

1 cup castor sugar
2/3 cup oil
2 eggs
1 tsp vanilla essence
1½ cups (180 gm) flour
1½ tsp baking powder
½ tsp baking soda (*mitha soda*)
1 tsp cinnamon
¼ tsp salt
1 cup grated carrots
1 cup drained and finely chopped tinned pineapple

Method

1. Stir together sugar and oil.

2. Stir in the eggs and vanilla, mix until well combined.

3. In a separate bowl, combine flour, baking powder, baking soda, cinnamon and salt.

4. Stir into sugar mixture just until well mixed.

5. Add carrots and pineapple. Mix lightly.

6. Spoon into greased muffin tin, filling ¾ full.

7. Bake in a preheated oven at 200ºC/400ºF for 20 minutes or until done.

8. Cool in pan for 5-10 minutes, then remove to a rack to finish cooling.

Lemon Poppy seed Cup cakes

Makes 12

Ingredients

½ cup unsalted butter, softened
¾ cup fine sugar
2 large eggs, separated
1⅓ cups flour
1 tsp baking powder
¾ tsp baking soda
¼ tsp salt
2 tbsp poppy seeds preferably black
½ cup buttermilk (⅓ cup milk mixed with 3 tbsp plain yogurt)
2 tbsp lemon juice and 1 tbsp lemon rind
1 tsp vanilla essence

Method

1. Preheat oven to 180°C/350°F. Line muffin tray with paper cups.

2. In a large bowl, cream the butter and sugar until fluffy.

3. Add the egg yolks, one at a time. Beat well after each addition.

4. In a separate bowl, stir together the dry ingredients, poppy seeds and lemon rind.

5. With the mixer on low speed, add the dry ingredients to the creamed mixture, alternating two times with the buttermilk, then lemon juice and then vanilla essence. Beat just until smooth.

6. In another bowl, beat the egg whites until soft peaks form.

7. Gently fold them into the cup cake batter until blended.

8. Spoon the batter into the prepared pan, fill ¾ of the tin. Bake at 180°C/350°F for 20-25 minutes or until a toothpick inserted in the center comes out clean. Cool for 5 minutes before removing to cool completely.

Mango Cup cakes with Mango Frost

Serves 12

Ingredients

1 cup fresh mango cubes - grind to get ½ cup mango puree
1½ cups flour (*maida*)
1 tsp baking powder
½ cup butter
1 cup fine sugar
1 large egg, 2 large egg whites
1 tsp vanilla essence (optional)

MANGO FROSTING
3 tbsp fresh mango puree
3 tbsp butter, 1 tbsp cheese spread
1½ cups icing sugar, or to taste
½ tsp mango essence, a few drops orange/yellow food colour

Method

1. Preheat oven to 180°C/350°F. Line muffin pan with paper cups.

2. In a medium bowl, combine flour amd baking powder and set aside.

3. Cream butter until lightly fluffy. Gradually add sugar and continue to whisk until well blended. Add one egg and egg whites and mix until lightly blended.

4. Add vanilla essence if using.

5. Alternately add flour and mango puree to the batter ending with flour. Scrape down sides of bowl and continue to blend well.

6. Using a ice-cream scoop or a tablespoon, add batter to prepared muffins cups. Bake for 20-25 minutes, or until lightly browned.

7. Cool cup cakes completely on a wire rack before adding the frosting.

8. To make the mango frosting, cream butter (soften) and cheese spread until fluffy. Add icing sugar and mix well. Add mango essence and 3 tbsp mango puree, mix till smooth. Add colour as desired.

9. Apply on cake with a help of a piping bag or a knife.

Note: In season fresh strawberry can be used instead of mango.

Date and Spice Cup cakes

Makes 18-20

Ingredients

85 gm flour (*maida*)
100 gm whole wheat flour (*atta*)
2 tsp baking powder
1 tsp ground mixed spice, given below
175 gm unsalted butter, softened
175 gm caster sugar
3 eggs
1 tsp vanilla essence
100 gm seedless dates, roughly chopped

Method

1. Preheat the oven at 160ºC/325ºF.

2. Sift the flours, baking powder and mixed spice into a large bowl, Add the butter sugar, eggs and vanilla essence. Beat well until the mixture is smooth, then stir in half the dates.

3. Spoon the mixture into the prepared cups and scatter over the remaining dates. Bake in the preheated oven for 20-25 minutes, or until risen and golden brown.

4. Leave to cool in the tin for 10 minutes, then turn out and finish cooling on a wire rack.

MIXED SPICE (CRUSH ALL TOGETHER)
2 cloves (*laung*)
1" cinnamon (*dalchini*)
seeds of 2 green cardamoms (*elaichi*)
½ star anise (*phool chakri*)

Almond Yogurt Cup cakes

Serves 10-12

Ingredients

175 gm flour (*maida*)
2 tbsp cornflour
1 tsp baking powder
125 gm plain yogurt
175 gm caster sugar
3 eggs
1 tsp vanilla essence
¼ cup oil
40 gm almonds - chopped

STRAWBERRY BUTTER CREAM
100 gm unsalted butter, softened
200 gm icing sugar
½ tsp strawberry essence
a drop of raspberry red colour
a few strawberries - sliced

Method

1. Preheat the oven to 190°C/375°F. Place paper cases into baking tray.

2. Sift the flour, cornflour and baking powder into a large bowl and add the yogurt, caster sugar, eggs, vanilla and oil. Beat well until the mixture is smooth, then stir in the chopped almonds.

3. Divide the mixture between the paper cups. Bake in he preheated oven for 20 minutes, or until risen, firm and golden brown. Transfer the cup cakes to a wire rack to cool.

4. For the topping, beat butter till smooth. Add the icing sugar gradually and beat until smooth. Add essence and colour. Pipe over the cup cakes and decorate with a fresh strawberry slice. Leave to set.

Orange and Peanut Cup cakes

Makes 18-20

Ingredients

1 firm orange
180 gm flour (*maida*)
1½ tsp baking powder
100 gm unsalted butter softened
70 gm crunchy peanut butter
175 gm caster sugar
3 eggs
1 tsp vanilla essence

ICING

½ cup peanut butter
2 tbsp orange juice
1 cup icing sugar
pinch of orange food colour

Method

1. Preheat the oven to 160ºC/325ºF. Line the tin with paper cups.

2. Grate the whole orange on a grater, without applying too much pressure, to get orange rind, see that only the top skin is grated without the white pith underneath it. Keep rind aside.

3. Separate the orange segments and remove the thin white skin. Cut into small chunks.

4. Sift the flour and baking powder into a large bowl and add the butter, peanut butter, caster sugar, eggs and vanilla essence. Beat well until the mixture is smooth.

5. Very gently, stir in the orange rind and orange chunks.

6. Spoon the mixture into the prepared cups. Bake in the preheated oven for 20-25 minutes, or until risen, firm and golden brown. Leave to cool in the tin for about 10 minutes, then turn out and finish cooling on a wire rack.

7. For the icing, mix together the peanut butter, orange juice, icing sugar and food colour, then spread over the cooled cup cakes with a table knife, picking up the frosting from the sides towards the centre to get the ruffled look.

Kiwi Cup cakes with Lemon Frosting

Makes 16-18

Ingredients

180 gm flour (*maida*)
1½ tsp baking powder
180 gm unsalted butter softened
180 gm caster sugar
3 eggs
1 tsp vanilla essence
2 kiwi fruit , peeled and chopped into ½" pieces

FROSTING
55 gm cream cheese
115 gm icing sugar
1 tbsp grated lemon rind
1 tsp lemon juice

Method

1. Preheat the oven to 160°C/325°F. Line the tin with paper cups.

2. Sift the flour and baking powder into a large bowl.

3. Add butter, caster sugar, eggs and vanilla essence. Beat well until the mixture is smooth, then stir in chopped kiwi fruit.

4. Spoon the mixture into the prepared tin. Bake in the preheated oven for about 25 minutes, or until risen, firm and golden brown.

5. Leave to cool in the tin for 10 minutes, then turn out and finish cooling on a wire rack.

6. For the frosting, beat together the cream cheese, lemon rind and icing sugar until smooth. Add lemon juice. Spread the frosting over the cup cakes and top with kiwi fruit slices.

Classic
BROWNIES

Traditional Chocolate Brownie

Makes 15

Ingredients

225 gm butter - cut into small pieces
150 gm dark cooking chocolate - chopped
175 gm brown sugar
225 gm flour (*maida*), ½ tsp baking powder
3 eggs
50 gm walnuts chopped, 100 gm dark chocolate chips

Method

1. Preheat the oven to 180°C/350°F. Grease and line a 9" square baking tin.

2. Put the butter and dark chocolate into a heat proof bowl set over a saucepan of gently simmering water (double boiler) until melted as on page 7. Remove from the heat.

3. Add brown sugar and beat with a beater till well mixed. Let it cool.

4. When the chocolate mixture is no longer hot, add the eggs to it and beat well.

5. Sift flour and baking powder into a mixing bowl. Add the chocolate-egg mix into the flour. Beat well. Add the nuts and chocolate chips and mix well. Spoon evenly into the prepared tin and level the surface.

6. Bake in the oven for 30 minutes, or until firm. To check whether the mixture is cooked through, insert a skewer into the centre-it should come out clean. If not, return the tin to the oven for a few minutes. Remove from the oven and leave to cool for 15 minutes. Turn out onto a wire rack to cool completely.

Cranberry & Almond Brownie

Makes 12-15

Ingredients

175 gm unsalted white butter
70 gm plain chocolate + 2 tbsp white butter
125 gm flour (*maida*)
½ tsp baking soda (*mitha soda*)
¼ tsp baking powder
100 gm brown sugar
50 gm almonds - roughly chopped
50 gm cranberry - chopped
½ tsp almond essence or vanilla essence
1 egg
2-3 tbsp milk

Method

1. Preheat the oven to 180°C/350°F. Grease and line a 11"×7" rectangular baking tin.

2. Put the chocolate and 2 tbsp white butter in a heatproof bowl set over a saucepan of gently simmering water and heat until it is melted as on page 7.

3. Meanwhile, sift together the flour, soda and baking powder in a large bowl.

4. In a separate bowl, cream together the butter and brown sugar, then mix in the essence and the egg.

5. Remove the chocolate from the heat and stir into the butter mixture.

6. Add the flour mixture, milk and chopped nuts and cranberries and stir until well combined.

7. Spoon the mixture into the prepared tin and smooth it. Transfer to the preheated oven and cook for 30 minutes, or until firm to the touch. Remove from the oven and leave to cool completely. Cut into 20 squares and serve.

Rich Apricot & Black Raisin Brownie

A white chocolate brownie with the richness of dry fruits.

Makes 8-10

Ingredients

250 gm white chocolate - chopped
85 gm unsalted butter
1tsp vanilla essence
2 eggs
100 gm brown sugar
115 gm flour (*maida*)
½ tsp baking powder
few almonds roughly chopped, optional
50 gm dried apricots - roughly chopped
50 gm dried black raisins or golden raisins

Method

1. Preheat the oven to 180°C/350°F. Lightly grease a 7" square baking tin and line the base with paper.

2. Chop half the white chocolate into small chunks. Melt the remaining white chocolate with the butter in a small heavy bottom pan over very low heat and stir until melted as on page 7. Remove from the heat and stir in the vanilla essence.

3. Beat the eggs and sugar together in a large bowl until pale. Beat in the melted chocolate mixture. Fold in the flour evenly with a spatula or spoon, then stir in the almonds, apricots, black currant and chopped white chocolate.

4. Spoon into the tin and smooth the top level. Bake for 30-35 minutes, or until firm and golden brown.

5. Leave to cool in the tin. Turn out when cold and cut into triangles or squares.

Mocha Brownie

Makes- 16

Ingredients

225 gm butter
115 gm plain chocolate - broken into pieces
225 gm caster sugar
2 eggs
3 tbsp instant coffee granules, dissolved in 4-5 tbsp hot water, cooled
225 gm flour
½ tsp baking powder (*maida*)
55 gm walnuts - roughly chopped

Method

1. Preheat the oven to 180°C/350°F. Grease and line the base of an 8" square baking tin.

2. Place the chocolate and butter in a heavy-based saucepan over a low heat until melted as on page 7. Stir and leave to cool.

3. Place the sugar and eggs in a large bowl and beat together until light and fluffy. Fold in the chocolate mixture and cooled coffee and mix thoroughly.

4. Sift flour and baking powder and lightly fold into the cake mixture. Carefully fold in the walnuts.

5. Pour the mixture into the prepared tin and bake in the preheated oven for 35-40 minutes, or until firm and a skewer inserted into the centre comes out clean.

6. Leave to cool in the tin for a few minutes, then run a knife around the edge of the cake to loosen it. Turn the cake out onto a wire rack and peel off the lining paper. Leave to cool completely. When cold, cut into squares.

Favourite
BROWNIES

White Chocolate Cherry Brownie

Makes 9

Ingredients

115 gm butter
175 gm white chocolate
75 gm walnut - chopped
2 eggs
115 gm caster sugar
115 gm flour (*maida*)
½ tsp baking powder
½ cup deseeded cherries

Method

1. Preheat the oven to 180°C/350°F. Lightly grease an 6"-7" square baking tin.

2. Coarsely chop 125 gm white chocolate and all the walnuts. Put the remaining (50 gm) chocolate and the butter in a heatproof bowl set over a saucepan of gently simmering water as on page 7. When melted, stir together, then set aside to cool slightly.

3. Beat the eggs and sugar together, then beat in the cooled chocolate mixture until well mixed. Fold in the flour, chopped chocolate and the walnuts. Turn the mixture into the prepared tin and smooth the surface, sprinkle the cherries.

4. Transfer the tin to the preheated oven and bake the brownies for about 30 minutes, until just set. The mixture should still be a little soft in the centre. Leave to cool in the tin, then cut into 9 squares before serving.

71

Marbled Choco Cheesecake Brownie

Makes-12

Ingredients

150 gm unsalted butter
3 tbsp cocoa
180 gm caster sugar
2 eggs
125 gm flour (*maida*)
¼ tsp baking powder

CHEESECAKE MIX

200 gm paneer
40 gm caster sugar
1 egg
½ tsp vanilla essence

Method

1. Preheat the oven to 180°C/350°F. Grease a 28×18 cm/11"×7" rectangular baking tin.

2. Melt the butter in a medium saucepan, remove from the heat and stir in the cocoa and sugar.

3. Add the eggs and beat well to mix.

4. Add the flour and baking powder and stir with a spatula or spoon to mix evenly. Pour into the prepared tin.

5. For the cheesecake mix - add paneer, sugar, vanilla and egg in a mixer and grind till smooth. Then drop teaspoonful of the mixture over the chocolate mixture. Use a knife to swirl the two mixtures together lightly.

6. Bake in the preheated oven for 40-45 minutes, until just firm to touch. Cool in the tin, then cut into bars or squares.

Chocolate Chip Brownie

Makes 12

Ingredients

225 gm butter, softened
150 gm dark cooking chocolate - cut into pieces
280 gm flour (*maida*)
150 gm caster sugar
4 eggs, beaten
100 gm dark or white chocolate chips
75 gm pistachio nuts (*pista*) - chopped, optional
icing sugar, for dusting (optional)

Method

1. Preheat the oven to 180°C/350°F. Lightly grease and line a 23 cm/9" square baking tin.

2. Melt chocolate and butter in a heatproof bowl set over a saucepan of gently simmering water (see page 7). Leave to cool slightly.

3. Sift the flour into separate mixing bowl and stir in the caster sugar.

4. Stir the eggs into the melted chocolate mixture, then pour this mixture into the flour and sugar mixture, beating well. Stir in the pistachio nuts and chocolate chips, then pour the mixture into the tin, spreading it evenly into the corners.

5. Bake in the preheated oven for 30-35 minutes, until firm to touch. Leave to cool in the tin for 20 minutes, then turn out onto a wire rack. Cut into 12 pieces and dust with icing sugar, if using.

Prune & Date Brownie

Makes 8-10

Ingredients

25 gm seedless dates - chopped
75 gm prunes - chopped
6 tbsp apple juice, readymade
4 medium eggs - beaten
½ cup oil
1 cup brown sugar
1 tsp vanilla essence
4 tbsp drinking chocolate powder
2 tbsp cocoa powder
1½ cups flour, ¼ tsp baking powder

Method

1. Preheat the oven to 180ºC/350ºF. Grease and line a 7" square cake pan with baking paper.

2. Place the dates and prunes in a small pan and add the apple juice. Bring to a boil, let simmer for 2-3 minutes until soft. Set aside to cool.

3. Place the cooled fruit in a mixing bowl. Add eggs, ½ cup oil, sugar and vanilla essence.

4. Sift drinking chocolate, cocoa, flour and baking powder. Add all this to the above mixture and stir gently with a spoon until everything is well combined.

5. Spoon the mixture into the pan and smooth over the top. Bake in the preheated oven, for 25-30 minutes, until firm to the touch or until a skewer inserted into the center comes out clean.

6. Cut into pieces and let cool in the pan for 10 minutes. Transfer to a wire rack to cool completely.

Double Chocolate Brownie

Makes 10

Ingredients

100 gm butter
115 gm cooking chocolate - cut into pieces
250 gm caster sugar
pinch of salt
1 tsp vanilla essence
2 large eggs
140 gm plain flour (*maida*)
2 tbsp cocoa powder
100 gm white/dark chocolate chips

FUDGE SAUCE, OPTIONAL
30 gm butter
120 gm caster sugar
200 ml cream
100 gm golden syrup/honey
100 gm milk/dark chocolate - cup into pieces

Method

1. Preheat the oven to 180°C/350°F. Grease and line the base of an 18 cm/7″ square baking tin.

2. Place the butter and chocolate in a small heatproof bowl set over a saucepan of gently simmering water until melted (see page 7). Stir until smooth. Leave to cool slightly.

3. Stir in the sugar, salt and vanilla essence.

4. Add the eggs, one at a time, and beat until well blended.

5. Sift the flour and cocoa powder and add into the mixture and beat until smooth. Stir in the chocolate chips, then pour the mixture into the tin. Bake in the preheated oven for 35-40 minutes, or until the top is evenly coloured and a skewer inserted into the centre comes out almost clean. Leave to cool slightly while preparing the sauce.

6. To make the sauce, place the butter, sugar, cream and syrup or honey in a small saucepan and heat gently until the sugar has dissolved. Bring to the boil and stir for 10 minutes, or until the mixture is caramel-coloured. Remove from the heat and add the chocolate. Stir until smooth. Cut the brownies into squares and serve immediately with the sauce.

Trendy
BROWNIES

Oat and Peanut Butter Brownie

Makes 10

Ingredients

150 gm flour (*maida*)
25 gm cocoa
½ tsp baking powder
100 gm butter, regular
125 gm brown sugar
80 gm quick cooking oats
50 gm chopped mixed nuts
2-3 tbsp milk
1 egg

TOPPING
35 gm crunchy peanut butter
200 gm condensed milk

Method

1. Preheat the oven to 180°C/350°F.

2. Sift the flour, cocoa and baking powder into a large bowl.

3. Add butter to the flour and rub in until the mixture resembles bread crumbs. Stir in the sugar, oats and half of the chopped nuts.

4. Put ¼ of the mixture into a bowl and add 2-3 tbsp milk to bind. Keep this aside for topping.

5. Stir the egg into the remaining ¾ of the mixture to get a soft dough. Press dough into the bottom of a 7" square baking tin. Bake the base in the preheated oven for 15 minutes.

6. Meanwhile, mix the condensed milk and peanut butter together. Pour the mixture over the baked base and spread evenly. Sprinkle the reserved topping mixture on the condensed milk mixture and press down lightly. Sprinkle the remaining nuts.

7. Return to the oven and bake for a further 25-30 minutes, until golden brown. Leave to cool in the tin, then cut into squares.

Upside-Down Apple Brownie Cake

Makes-9

Ingredients

APPLE TOPPING
85 gm brown sugar
55 gm unsalted butter
1 apple, cored and thinly sliced

BROWNIE CAKE
115 gm unsalted butter, plus extra for greasing
175 gm brown sugar
2 eggs beaten
200 gm flour (*maida*)
1 tsp baking powder
½ tsp baking soda (*mitha soda*)
1 tsp ground mixed spice, given below
2 apples - peeled and coarsely grated
85 gm roasted chopped peanuts

Method

1. Preheat the oven to 180ºC/350ºF. Grease 9" round baking tin.

2. For the topping, place the sugar and butter in a small pan and heat gently, stirring, until melted. Pour into the prepared tin. Arrange the apple slices over the mixture.

3. For the brownie cake, place the butter and sugar in a bowl and beat well until pale and fluffy. Beat in the eggs gradually.

4. Sift together the flour, baking powder, baking soda and mixed spice, and fold into the mixture, stir in the apples and nuts.

5. Pour into the prepared tin and bake for 35-40 minutes, until firm and golden. Cool in the tin for 10 minutes, then turn out and cut into pieces.

MIXED SPICE (CRUSH ALL TOGETHER)
2 cloves (*laung*)
1" cinnamon (*dalchini*)
seeds of 2 green cardamoms (*elaichi*)
½ star anise (*phool chakri*)

Chocolate Fudge Brownie

Makes 20 squares

Ingredients

225 gm unsalted butter
150 gm dark cooking chocolate - cut into small pieces
200 gm brown sugar
100 gm caster sugar
4 eggs
150 gm flour (*maida*)
25 gm cocoa powder
¼ tsp baking powder
1 tsp vanilla essence
½ tsp salt
75 gm walnuts - cut into small pieces

FOR TOPPING

50 gm milk chocolate - cut into small pieces
25 gm unsalted butter
90 gm icing sugar
2-3 tbsp water
50 gm finely chopped walnuts

Method

1. Preheat oven at 180°C/350°F. Line and grease a 10" x 7" baking tin.

2. Sieve flour, cocoa and baking powder together.

3. Melt butter. Switch off the gas and add dark chocolate (should be cut finely so that it melts uniformly). Stir in the sugars and mix well. Let the mixture cool down. Add the eggs, one at a time and whisk on, ensuring they are thoroughly incorporated.

4. Sieve flour mixture into the egg mixture and fold using a spatula. Add the vanilla essence and salt.

5. Add finely cut milk chocolate and walnuts to the batter. Spoon into prepared tin, smooth top and bake for 40 minutes or until cooked.

6. To make topping, melt butter and add cut milk chocolate. Remove from heat and stir until melted, add the icing sugar and whisk until smooth. Add sufficient water to give a spreading consistency and spread over the top of the brownie. Sprinkle walnuts. Leave to set for 30 minutes.

White Brownie with Toffee Sauce

Makes 9

Ingredients

200 gm white chocolate
75 gm butter
75 gm walnut pieces
2 eggs
75 gm caster sugar
115 gm flour (*maida*), ½ tsp baking powder

NUTTY TOFFEE SAUCE

90 gm caster sugar, 25 gm white butter, 2 tbsp hot water
25 ml fresh cream, 1½ tbsp condensed milk (milk maid)
½ cup roasted mix chopped nuts (walnuts, almonds, peanuts and cashew)

Method

1. Preheat the oven to 180°C/350°F. Lightly grease an 18 cm/7" square baking tin.

2. Coarsely chop 150 gm of the chocolate and all the walnuts. Put the remaining (50 gm) chocolate and the butter in a heatproof bowl set over a saucepan of gently simmering water as on page 7. When melted, stir together, then set aside to cool slightly.

3. Beat the eggs and sugar together, then beat in the cooled chocolate mixture until well mixed.

4. Fold in the flour, chopped chocolate and the walnuts using a spatula. Turn the mixture into the prepared tin and smooth the surface.

5. Transfer the tin to the preheated oven and bake the brownies for about 30 minutes, until just set. The mixture should still be a little soft in the centre. Leave to cool in the tin.

6. For the toffee sauce, heat a flat non stick pan. Add sugar and keep on medium heat till sugar starts to melt on the sides. Reduce heat and swirl the pan 2-3 times in between to melt sugar uniformly. Keep on low heat till it melts completely and turns very light brown. Do not use a spoon.

7. Reduce heat and add 2 tbsp hot water and butter together. Mix vigorously with a spoon for a minute till smooth.

8. Remove from fire. Add cream and mix till blended. Return to fire.

9. Add milkmaid. Mix and cook for about 1-2 minutes on low flame till it turns thick, starts leaving the pan and turns a little sticky like toffee when felt between the thumb and finger. Add nuts and cool slightly and spread on the brownie.

Mochachino Brownie Cake

Makes 8-9

Ingredients

80 gm unsalted butter
115 gm plain chocolate
3 tsp coffee powder - dissolved in 2 tbsp hot water
125 gm caster sugar
½ tsp ground cinnamon
3 eggs
100 gm plain flour (*maida*), 1 tsp baking powder
55 gm white chocolate chips, 50 gms walnuts - chopped
8-10 nutties and chocolate curls to decorate

WHITE MOCHA SAUCE
100 ml cream
85 gm white chocolate
1 tsp coffee powder - dissolved in 1 tbsp hot water

Method

1. Preheat the oven to 180°C/350°F. Grease and line a 8" round or 9" square baking tin.

2. Place the butter, chocolate and coffee in a medium saucepan over a low heat and stir until just melted and smooth. Cool slightly.

3. Whisk in the sugar, cinnamon and eggs. Beat in the flour, baking powder, chocolate chips and walnuts. Pour into the prepared tin.

4. Bake in the oven for 30-35 minutes, until just firm but still moist inside. Let it cool.

5. Meanwhile, make the sauce by placing all the ingredients in a small pan over a low heat, stirring occasionally, until melted and smooth.

6. Place the brownies on plate and spread the warm sauce on top. Decorate with curls and nutties. Cut into pieces and serve.

Oreo Fudge Brownie

Makes 16

Ingredients

85 gm butter
3 tbsp cocoa powder
75 gm paneer, 2-3 tbsp milk
25 gm cheese spread
½ tsp vanilla essence
175 gm caster sugar
2 eggs
100 gm flour (*maida*), sifted
5-6 oreo cookies - broken into small pieces

FUDGE FROSTING
55 gm butter, 1 tbsp milk
75 gm icing sugar, 2 tbsp cocoa powder
oreo cookies - broken into small pieces, for decoration

Method

1. Preheat the oven to 180°C/350°F. Lightly grease 8" square baking tin and line the base with paper.

2. Grind paneer and cheese spread in a mixer to get a smooth mixture. Add 2-3 tbsp milk if the mixture appears too thick and grind again till smooth and soft.

3. Beat together the cheese-paneer mixture, vanilla essence and 5 tsp of caster sugar until smooth, mix the cookies gently and set the mixture aside.

4. Beat the eggs and remaining caster sugar together until and fluffy. Place the butter and cocoa powder in a small pan and heat gently, stirring until the butter melts and the mixture combines, cool and then stir it into the egg mixture. Fold in the flour and nuts.

5. Pour half of the mixture into the tin and smooth the top. Carefully spread the cheese mixture over it, then cover it with the remaining mixture. Bake in the preheated oven for 40-45 minutes. Let cool in the tin.

6. For the fudge frosting, melt butter and milk in a small pan. Stir in the icing sugar and cocoa powder. Spread the frosting over the brownies and decorate with oreo cookies. Let the frosting set, then cut into squares to serve.

Cocktail Brownie With Rum Sauce

Makes 8-10

Ingredients

100 gm butter
115 gm dark cooking chocolate
½ tsp coarsely ground black peppercorns (*saboot kali mirch*)
2 eggs
175 gm caster sugar
½ tsp vanilla essence
3 tbsp rum
2 tbsp vodka
150 gm flour (*maida*)
¼ tsp baking powder
55 gm chopped walnuts, plus extra to decorate

RUM SAUCE
1 cup water, ¼ cup brown sugar, 1 tbsp cornflour
2-3 tbsp butter, 1 tsp cofee powder
2 tbsp rum, ½ tsp lemon juice

Method

1. Preheat the oven to 180°C/350°F. Grease and line the base of 7-8" square baking tin.

2. Melt the chocolate and the butter with the peppercorns in a small saucepan over a low heat. Remove from the heat and cool slightly.

3. Beat together the eggs, sugar and vanilla essence in a large bowl and stir in the chocolate mixture, rum and vodka.

4. Sift the flour and baking powder and stir evenly into the chocolate mixture. Stir in the walnuts. Pour into the tin and bake in the oven for 20-25 minutes, until just firm to the touch.

5. Cool for a few minutes, then cut into bars or squares and lift carefully from the tin onto serving plates. Spoon the rum sauce over the squares.

6. For rum sauce, mix sugar and cornflour with water and cook over low heat, stirring till it coats the spoon, about 5 minutes. Add coffee to taste. Remove from fire. Add 2-3 tbsp butter. Add rum and few drops of lemon juice.

Mint Brownie with Mint sauce

Makes 6-8

Ingredients

100 gm unsalted butter, 125 gm flour (*maida*)
150 gm chocolate, 2 eggs, 150 gm brown sugar
3 tbsp brandy or rum or 1 tsp vanilla essence
1 tbsp chopped fresh mint, mint springs to decorate

SAUCE
100 gm white or dark chocolate, preferably white
100 ml cream, ¼ tsp peppermint essence

Method

1. Preheat the oven to 180°C/350°F. Grease and flour a 7" square baking tin. Dust with flour.

2. Place the chocolate and butter in a pan over a very low heat and stir occasionally until melted as given on page 7. Remove from heat.

3. Beat together the eggs, sugar, brandy and chopped mint, then beat quickly into the chocolate mixture. Fold in the flour and mix evenly.

4. Pour the mixture into the prepared tin and smooth the surface. Bake in the oven for 30-35 minutes, until just firm, but still slightly soft inside.

5. Allow to cool in the tin for 15 minutes, then remove from the tin.

6. For the sauce, place the chocolate, cream and peppermint extract in a small pan and heat gently, stirring, until melted and smooth.

7. To serve, place the brownies on serving plates, drizzle with the chocolate sauce and decorate with springs of mint.

Gluten Free
RECIPES

Vanilla Cup cakes

Makes 12-15

Ingredients

½ cup butter
1 cup icing sugar
4 eggs
2 tsp vanilla
1 cup cornflour
1¼ tsp baking powder

Method

1. Preheat oven to 190ºC/375ºF. Line a muffin pan with paper cups.

2. In a large bowl cream butter and sugar.

3. Add the eggs and vanilla. Beat until light and fluffy.

4. In a small bowl mix the cornflour and baking powder together and fold slowly into the creamed mixture.

5. Mix until well blended.

6. Fill the lined muffin tins half full.

7. Bake for 15 minutes or till done.

8. Remove from the pan while still warm. Let them cool.

9. Serve topped with strawberries and whipped cream or any frosting.

Peanut & Honey Cup cakes

Makes 6-8

Ingredients

60 gm butter
50 gm honey
2 eggs
1 tsp vanilla essence
100 gm caster sugar
100 gm roasted peanuts
30 gm rice flour
1 tsp baking powder

Method

1. Grind peanuts to a rough powder, churning the mixer just for a few seconds. Scrape down the sides and churn again. Do not let it turn to a paste by grinding too much.

2. Mix together the rice flour, ground peanuts and baking powder. Keep aside.

3. Beat butter and sugar till light and fluffy, Beat eggs into the mixture.

4. Add honey and vanilla essence.

5. Gently fold the dry ingredients into the butter-sugar mixture with a spatula. Transfer to a muffin pan lined with paper cups. Bake for 15 minutes at 190°C/375°F.

Almond Flour Brownie

Makes 10-12

Ingredients

60 gm butter
150 gm dark chocolate
1 tsp strong instant coffee
1 tsp vanilla essence
100 gm ground almonds
75 gm caster sugar, 2 eggs, separated
icing sugar, to decorate (optional)

Method

1. Preheat the oven to 180°C/350°F. Line and grease a 6" square baking tin with paper.

2. Melt the chocolate and butter in a heatproof bowl placed over a saucepan of gently simmering water, making sure that the bottom of the bowl does not touch the water. See page 7. Stir very occasionally until the chocolate and butter have melted and are smooth.

3. Carefully remove the bowl from the heat. Leave to cool slightly, then stir in the coffee and vanilla essence. Add the almonds and sugar and mix well until combined. Lightly beat the egg yolks in a separate bowl, then stir into the chocolate mixture.

4. Whisk the egg whites in a large bowl until they form stiff peaks. Gently fold a large spoonful of the egg whites into the chocolate mixture, then fold in the reminder until completely incorporated.

5. Spoon the mixture into the prepared tin and bake in the preheated oven for 35-40 minutes, or until risen and firm on top but still slightly gooey in the centre. Leave to cool in the tin, then turn out, remove the lining paper and cut into 12 pieces. Dust with icing sugar before serving, if using.

Rice Flour Brownie

Makes 24

Ingredients

> 1/3 cup butter
> 1 cup light brown sugar, firmly packed
> 2 eggs, lightly beaten
> 200 gm semi-sweet chocolate, melted, see page 7
> 1 tsp vanilla
> 2/3 cup rice flour
> ½ tsp baking powder
> ¼ tsp salt
> ½ cup almonds or ½ cup walnuts, coarsely chopped

Method

1. In a medium bowl beat butter and sugar until creamy.

2. Add all the remaining ingredients except the nuts and keep blending until mixture is very smooth.

3. Stir in the nuts and pour into a greased 8"×8" or 9"×9" pan.

4. Bake about 30 minutes at 180ºC/350ºF or until the sides shrink a little from the side of the pan and the top springs back when touched.

5. Cool in the pan on a wire rack. Cut into squares.

Baking Powder

A raising agent consisting of 2 parts cream of tartar to 1 part bicarbonate soda. It is effected by heat and moisture and reacts to produce carbon dioxide gas, which is trapped within the protein structure of the product which is being baked.

Baking Soda

Sodium bi-carbonate, see Bicarbonate of soda.

Bicarbonate of Soda

Is also known in some countries as baking soda. It is usually used as a raising agent for cakes, pastries and breads.

Brown Sugar

Is a coarse crystal sugar and as the natural colouring of the raw sugar has not been removed, it retains its light brown colour. Also called Demerara sugar.

Caster Sugar

Very finely granulated table sugar. You can grind granulated sugar at home and use as caster sugar. It dissolves quickly when creamed with butter.

Cream of Tartar

The chemical name is potassium acid tartrate. It is a fine white powder, which collects in the bottom of cases, in which grapes have fermented. It is refined and sold either by itself or as an ingredient in the raising agent called baking powder. Baking powder can be used as a substitute.

Cointreau, Liqueur

Citrus-flavoured liqueur.

Corn syrup

Available light or dark, liquid glucose can be substituted.

Cream

Milk fat. Single cream has 18% fat content, whipping cream has 38% fat and double cream 48% fat.

Crème de Cacao, liqueur

Chocolate-flavour liqueur.

Demerara Sugar

Is a coarse crystal sugar and as the natural colouring of the raw sugar has not been removed, it retains its light brown colour. Also called brown sugar.

Flour

Is included in most of the recipes, either plain flour (*maida*) or whole wheat (*atta*). Always make it a habit to sift flour once or twice is even better. The reason why the amount of liquid required to bind ingredients together can alter slightly is due to the type of flour.

Food Colourings

Available in liquid, powder or paste form.

Grand Marnier, Liqueur

Orange-based liqueur based on cognac.

Golden Syrup

By product of sugar, pure maple syrup or honey can be substituted.

Icing Sugar

Also known as confectioners sugar. Superfine powdered sugar with addition of 3% cornflour. Used mainly for icing cakes and pastries. Icing sugar gives a softer finish when dusted over the top of cakes and biscuits.

Kahlua, Liqueur

Coffee-flavoured liqueur.

Kirsch, Liqueur

Cherry-flavoured liqueur.

Praline

Sugar is caramelized and almonds added to it. When the caramelized sugar sets, the almonds coated with the golden sugar are crushed to a coarse powder known as praline. Useful in adding texture and flavour to butter cream and cake fillings, or as decoration.

Self Raising Flour

Self raising flour already contains raising agents and so baking powder must only be used when specified. Self raising flour has 1 tsp baking powder added to each cup of flour. The raising agents are evenly blended within the flour and so it eliminates errors.

Whipping Cream

Is a lighter version of double cream, with at least 35% fat content and whips easily without the richness. Excellent as a pouring cream or for swirling on desserts.

Baking powder lying in the cupboard since many days...

Keep replacing baking powder and baking soda (*mitha soda*) after every 5-6 months. Before buying baking powder, check the manufacturing date. Baking powder stays good for a year only. To check if it is effective, put ½ tsp in a cup of hot water. If bubbles form, it is usable, if no bubbles, discard!

INTERNATIONAL CONVERSION GUIDE

These are not exact equivalents; they've been rounded-off to make measuring easier.

WEIGHTS & MEASURES

Metric	Imperial
15 g	½ oz
30 g	1 oz
60 g	2 oz
90 g	3 oz
125 g	4 oz (¼ lb)
155 g	5 oz
185 g	6 oz
220 g	7 oz
250 g	8 oz (½ lb)
280 g	9 oz
315 g	10 oz
345 g	11 oz
375 g	12 oz (¾ lb)
410 g	13 oz
440 g	14 oz
470 g	15 oz
500 g	16 oz (1 lb)
750 g	24 oz (1 ½ lb)
1 kg	30 oz (2 lb)

LIQUID MEASURES

Metric	Imperial
30 ml	1 fluid oz
60 ml	2 fluid oz
100 ml	3 fluid oz
125 ml	4 fluid oz
150 ml	5 fluid oz (¼pint/ 1 gill)
190 ml	6 fluid oz
250 ml	8 fluid oz
300 ml	10 fluid oz (½ pint)
500 ml	16 fluid oz
600 ml	20 fluid oz (1 pint)
1000 ml	1¾ pints

CUPS & SPOON MEASURES

Metric	Imperial
1 ml	¼ tsp
2 ml	½ tsp
5 ml	1 tsp
15 ml	1 tbsp
60 ml	¼ cup
125 ml	½ cup
250 ml	1 cup

HELPFUL MEASURES

Metric	Imperial
3 mm	1/8 in
6 mm	¼ in
1 cm	½ in
2 cm	¾ in
2.5 cm	1 in
5 cm	2 in
6 cm	2½ in
8 cm	3 in
10 cm	4 in
13 cm	5 in
15 cm	6 in
18 cm	7 in
20 cm	8 in
23 cm	9 in
25 cm	10 in
28 cm	11 in
30 cm	12 in (1 ft)

HOW TO MEASURE

When using the graduated metric measuring cups, it is important to shake the dry ingredients loosely into the required cup. Do not tap the cup on the table, or pack the ingredients into the cup unless otherwise directed. Level top of cup with a knife. When using graduated metric measuring spoons, level top of spoon with a knife. When measuring liquids in the jug, place jug on a flat surface, check for accuracy at eye level.

OVEN TEMPERATURE

These oven temperatures are only a guide.

	°C (Celsius)	°F (Fahrenheit)	Gas Mark
Very low	120	250	1
Low	150	300	2
Moderately low	160	325	3
Moderate	180	350	4
Moderately high	190	375	5
High	200	400	6
Very high	230	450	7

BEST SELLING COOKBOOKS BY

Shakes Smoothies & Desserts

Street Food of Delhi

Sizzlers Cookbook

Best of Chicken & Paneer

Amritsari Khaana

Wraps Rolls & Sandwiches

Chicken Snacks & Salads

Mexican Vegetarian Cooking

Vegetarian Snacks

Learn to Cook Chinese - Vegetarian

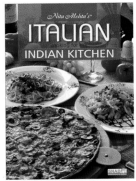

Italian cooking for the Indian kitchen

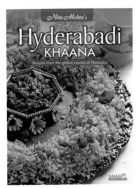

HYDERABADI Khaana

Eggless Cakes & Muffins

Microwave Desi Khaana

Continental cooking for the Indian kitchen

101 Diet Recipes

BEST SELLING COOKBOOKS BY

Cookbook of Regional Cuisine of India

Un-fried & Baked Snacks

Different ways with Paneer

Cookbook of Rajasthan

Cookbook for Festivals of India

Indian Cooking with Olive Oil

Permanent Weight Loss Cookbook

Traditional & Innovative MITHAI

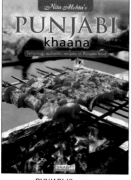

PUNJABI Khaana

Learn to Cook Pizza & Pasta

Snacks for Children

Bakes & Cakes

101 Chicken Recipes

Step by Step Chocolate Cookbook

Zero Oil Cooking

Cakes & Cake Decorations

BEST SELLING COOKBOOKS BY

Fish & Prawns

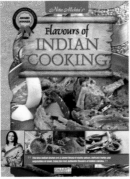

Flavours of Indian Cooking

Mother & Child Cookbook

Best of Indian Cooking

Different ways with Pasta

Soups & Salads

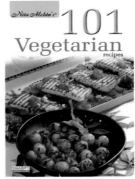

101 Vegetarian Recipes

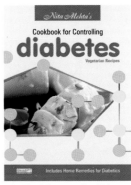

Cookbook for controlling Diabetes

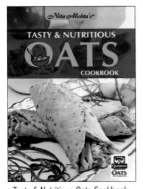

Tasty & Nutritious Oats Cookbook

Cooking for Growing Children

101 Recipes for Children

Asian Cookbook

Step by Step Food for Children

Step by Step Soups & Salads

Permanent way to Good Health

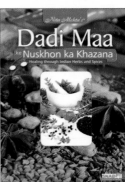

Dadi Maa Ke Nuskhon Ka Khazana